TWENTY-ONE DAYS TO LOVING ME

Lisa Knowles-Smith

Book Cover Designed By Evo World Design

www.evoworldent.com/

PATASKITY PUBLISHING CO.

Published By Pataskity Publishing Company

Pataskity Publishing (USA) LLC.

www.Pataskitypublishing.com

Copyright © 2021 Lisa Knowles-Smith. All rights reserved. No portion of this book may be reproduced mechanically, electronically, or by any other means, including photocopying, without the author's written permission. It is illegal to copy this book, post it on a website, or distribute it by any other means without permission from the author.

Table of Contents

DAY ONE 1
TOPIC: IF LOVING ME IS WRONG, I DON'T WANT TO BE RIGHT! 1

DAY TWO 4
TOPIC: LOVE IS WHAT LOVE DOES 4

DAY THREE 7
TOPIC: LOVE, A WORD THAT COMES AND GOES 7

DAY FOUR 10
TOPIC: FALLING IN AND OUT OF LOVE 10

DAY FIVE 14
LOVE DON'T COST A THING 14

DAY SIX 17
TOPIC: LOVE IS PATIENT, LOVE IS KIND 17

DAY SEVEN 20
TOPIC: LOVE NEVER FAILS 20

DAY EIGHT 23
TOPIC: LOVE GIVES LIFE 23

DAY NINE 26
TOPIC: REALLY; WHAT DOES LOVE HAVE TO DO WITH IT? 26

DAY TEN 29
TOPIC: MAKE LOVE, NOT WAR! 29

DAY ELEVEN 32

Topic: I Just Called To Say, "I love you!" 32

DAY TWELVE **35**
Topic: Love Stinks! 35

DAY THIRTEEN **38**
Topic: Live, Laugh & Love 38

DAY FOURTEEN **42**
Topic: Love Versus Like 42

DAY FIFTEEN **46**
Topic: Love To Hate 46

DAY SIXTEEN **49**
Topic: Lovely Day 49

DAY SEVENTEEN **52**
Topic: Love On Top 52

DAY EIGHTEEN **55**
Topic: Love Heals 55

DAY NINETEEN **58**
Topic: Beloved 58

DAY TWENTY **61**
Topic: An Overflow Of Love 61

DAY TWENTY ONE **64**
Topic: Loving Me Better 64

Day One

Topic: If Loving Me Is Wrong, I Don't Want To Be Right!

"I will praise thee; for I am fearfully and wonderfully made: marvelous are thy works; and that my soul knoweth right well."
Psalms 139:14 KJV

Have you ever experienced someone who gave, but failed in ever learning how to reciprocate? Sometimes people put themselves last while others are compelled with greed, and always put themselves first. Whenever we put others before ourselves, it is often because we hope by doing so that it would create a continuous cycle and reciprocity of love. This is not only a false belief, but it is also a misleading perception of love.

Love is not only to be given, but also received. Love becomes more of a treasure when it is reciprocal. However, in most instances, we find that we put other people's desires in life before our own, because we think they will love us less if we don't do what they desire of us. While I find this type of behavior to be common, it is incorrect. Because you put yourself first, people may say, "*You are being selfish.*" They may fail to understand that self-love is the initial meaning of love. In further explanation, Hebrew is the original language of the Bible. Let's look at the meaning of love in the Hebrew content. The word love in Hebrew is *Ahava* which means *I give*. Since *love* means *I give*, it has to be given and shared. We must share love with ourselves before we can share it with anyone else. While love is not love until we have taken it and given it away, it does not always have to be physical or monetary giving, we can choose to give spiritual support, time and prayers. Don't go bankrupt trying to love someone else, and you have failed to give love to yourself.

God loves everything about you, so of course, it is his will that you grow in peace and love how wonderful and marvelous you are. Yes, I said wonderful and marvelous. It is perfectly fine with the Father if you love yourself! Feeling unloved is not a good feeling! If you are not good, nothing around you is good.

Think about it, when you are good, life in every capacity is good. You have to take on the responsibility to love yourself FIRST! Self- love is the beginning of love for any human being.

Questions:

1. What are some ways that you can love yourself?
2. Why shouldn't you feel bad about loving yourself?
3. What do you hope that others will get from you loving yourself?

Day Two

Topic: Love Is What Love Does

"For God so loved the world, that he gave his only begotten Son, that whosoever believeth in him should not perish, but have everlasting life."

John 3:16 KJV

As we discovered on Day One, love is truth, and means, I give. Truth is "love" is an action word! It is so easy to say, "*I love you.*" It is even better to say, "*I love myself.*" While God loved us with an eternal, everlasting love, He is the only one who can love us with this type of Agape Love. God's love is for humanity, but it is not at all humanistic. We love with conditions and terms; however, God does not. In Romans 5:8, Apostle Paul teaches us about God's Agape Love. He wrote "But God commanded his Love (Agape) toward us, in that while we were yet sinners, Christ died for us;" Agape Love counts no wrong, and is the type of Love that God gives ongoing. While we are to love people, only God can love beyond our understanding.

Here's where it gets interesting, what do you do to show that you love others or yourself. Whenever I think of showing love to myself, I think of taking care of myself. Simple things like going to the doctor to get checkups. I think of grooming. I think of being open to being cultured and free. Most importantly, I think of being connected to the creator. It's important as believers that we understand and believe what the Word of God says about us and life.

God literally left us a book of instructions to help us along life's journey. The book gives us examples to follow and shows us the way. Why wouldn't you want to follow the instructions? For instance, have you ever bought a bookcase, opened the box and there's a million pieces because you have to assemble it. I know, we all dread it. All of these pieces that look exactly the same or similar, five of this piece and twenty-five of this or that. Just looking at the pieces trying to figure it out is so frustrating, but if you just read the instructions it will tell you where everything goes. Suddenly, all of these pieces begin to make sense.

That's very similar to our lives, the best way to love yourself is to follow the instructions God created for your life! Remember, the Creator has all of the instructions and He knows best.

Questions:

1. What are some ways that you show love to yourself?
2. What are some ways that you show love to others?
3. Evaluate your life. Are you connected to the creator? Explain why or why not.

Day Three

Topic: Love, A Word That Comes And Goes

"And now these three remain: faith, hope and love. But the greatest of these is love."
1 Corinthians 13:13 NIV

I can recall watching movies and laughing at people referring to the word love as the "l" word. It was not only funny but also profound that a word had so much power they could not even say it. Recalling these memories brings me to this point, nowadays people often use the word *love* so freely, but do not really understand the meaning of it. As in Day One, let's further examine the definition of love.

love

/lʌv/

noun

1. an intense feeling of deep affection."babies fill parents with intense feelings of love"

2. a person or thing that one loves.

"she was the love of his life"

verb

1. feel a deep romantic or sexual attachment to (someone)."do you love me?"

Whenever I think of the word love, I think of the difference between liking something and loving it. There is a huge difference between the things that I like and the things that I love. The things that I like I can do without, but when you love something, the chances are you would rather have it.

Not to sound harsh, but sometimes a person's behavior may not appeal to me. In return, I love them, but I may not like their ways or behavior which causes them to not be a necessity in my life. However, there are people who are essential to my life, and contribute greatly to who I am as a woman. For example, I love (Philos and Eros) my husband and I don't want to be without him. Philos means that he is my closest friend, and eros meaning that he is the love of my life. This is the order of love that God instructed:

1. Love Christ
2. Self-Love
3. Spouse
4. Children
5. Family, friends, and others

Ultimately, I must also love myself! I can't live without me. Don't leave yourself out. Love yourself! Sharing love or giving love is a wonderful gesture, but you have to be sure to love you!

Questions:

1. Have you reviewed the definitions of love? If so, explain how you define love?
2. Have you ever given more love than you received? If so, explain.
3. What is the difference between self-love and agape love?

Day Four

Topic: Falling In And Out Of Love

"Above all, love each other deeply, because love covers over a multitude of sins."

1 Peter 4:8 NIV

Nowadays, it is possible to fall in and out of love. I used to have a friend who had a different boyfriend every month. That was cool until she was in love with them. I would think to myself, *"How can she possibly be in love with different men at the same time?"* The answer is simple! What she felt for these men was not love at all. Her idea of love was as twisted as many people of today's society. Love was not the problem; it was her idea of it that was an issue. As we revisit the scripture once more, *Ludas* is a meaning of love in Greek. Ludas means an un-committed type of love. For example, you may recall the story of

Amon and his half-sister, Tamar. Amnon raped Tamar and when she begged for a marriage, the scriptures state in 2 Samuel 13:15 that he hated her more than he had ever loved her, "Then Amnon hated her with intense hatred. In fact, he hated her more than he had loved her. Amnon said to her, "Get up and get out!" What a twisted type of love!

My husband once preached a sermon "*What's Love Got To Do With It?*" In his sermon, he touched on psychological drives, love being one. The theory suggests that drive can alter your behavior until the need of the drive has been fulfilled. So, for instance, if you are hungry, you will eat until you are full. So, if the desire is love, you date, kiss, have intercourse or whatever until the need is fulfilled. Problem is we confuse love with lust. Ludas, again means lust, and the desire to only serve the appetite for the time being. Unfortunately, many people fall into what they think is love, but it is not love. These feelings are twisted, not sincere, and only temporary.

Ludas (lustful love) is a feeling that at times feels uncontrollable. Agape, eros or even Philos love is intentional and is birthed from a place of truly loving yourself. My theory is that the only way you can fall in and out of love with someone is because you are falling in and out of love with yourself. Will you be able to love another person as much as you love yourself?

As Christians, we are taught about ourselves as the embodiment of God's perfect love expressed through his son. We know that "...as he is, so as we are also in this world" (1 John 4:17). This is the perfection of God's love for us. So, in loving ourselves, we are not just loving our human self, we are loving the fullness of God in us; we are basking in who He is in us. That is why John could boldly say we love him because he first loved us. In light of this truth, we are able to love God, and in return love ourselves. And when we love ourselves, we can truly love others and not switch how we feel for what love truly is: sacrifice and intentionality. It is important to know love is always a choice that we make, and when we make the choice to love, love is always intentional.

Questions:

1. Did you know that in Hebrew/ Greek love has many meanings?
2. Have you ever experienced a twisted feeling that you thought was love?
3. What type of love does God have towards us, his children?

Day Five

Love Don't Cost A Thing

"We love because He first loved us."

1 John 4:19 NIV

I often think about God loving us so much that He sent His only son to pay the price for our sins! God's Agape love is the perfect example of sacrificial natural love. God, in His wisdom, realized that we cannot, by ourselves, love people the best way, so He decided to show us what love is. He died. His death was more than just an example; it is the foundation of love.

John writes about how our love is not dependent on our abilities to love right, but on God's already established love. We are not judged by our abilities to love, but on the Lord's love for us. We draw our 'loving' strength from His love. Love doesn't cost a thing... if you realize how much God's love strengthens you to love like Him. Remember, we said in Day One that God's love is for humanity but not humanistic.

When the scripture says, 'It is God who works in you both to will and to do His Good pleasures" (Phi 2:13), it means that our abilities to do right and love right is not dependent on us. We must pray to love ourselves. We must pray to even like ourselves in moments when we make mistakes. We also should forgive ourselves. Forgiveness is one key to falling in love with you! Love and forgiveness are interlinked.

The Bible teaches us about how Jesus taught his disciples to forgive. In Matthew chapter 18, the story of the disciples asking Jesus about forgiveness is told. "Then came Peter to him, and said, Lord, how often shall my brother sin against me, and I forgive him? till seven times?" (Matthew 18:21) Jesus' reply was phenomenal. Seventy times seven times! Jesus replied. The disciples were shocked. Fall in love with yourself daily. Forgive yourself daily. Be patient with yourself. Be kind to yourself! After all, because of Calvary, love is free and is available to you.

Questions:

1. Do you know that loving yourself is free?
2. Have you forgiven yourself lately?
3. What are sweet or kind gestures that you do for yourself?
4. Explain how treating yourself kindly makes you feel better.

Day Six

Topic: Love Is Patient, Love Is Kind

"Love is patient, love is kind. It does not envy, it does not boast, it is not proud. It does not dishonor others, it is not self-seeking, it is not easily angered, it keeps no record of wrongs."

1 Corinthians 13:4-5 NIV

This scripture is the hallmark of God's definition of love. Have you ever thought about practicing each of these behaviors with yourself? Perhaps being patient with yourself, not envying others because of what you feel you lack, and learning how to be content with yourself. Have you looked in the mirror lately, and thought to yourself, *"Hey you! I am keeping no records of your wrongs. I won't hold your failures against you."* As odd as it may seem, many of you have not. Have you lacked in loving yourself? Amazingly, Christ taught us to love others, but the expectation is that you would have at least gotten to know and love yourself. Practice 1st Corinthians 13 with others, but again, do not leave yourself out!

People have misconstrued love so much that many have stopped believing in love. On social media, many young people – and older ones too – have stopped believing in the existence of love and its authenticity. You'll read things such as *"there is no love in these streets."* How can we lose belief in something so beautiful as love? The stories they've heard and read on social media and from close friends made them stop believing in the beauty of love. You may even wonder, *"What are we to believe about love as Christians?"* Because the definition of love has become so tainted, it is easy for anyone to wonder. "But God, who is rich in mercy, for his great love wherewith he loved us...(Ephesians 2:4). We see from this verse that God is the author of love for us. When we were children, we often joked about Jesus' parable of turning the other cheek after we have been slapped. We laughed at the parable because we felt it was impossible for anyone to be so 'stupid' as to turn their other cheek after they've just been slapped. While that parable was not literal, it exemplifies the type of love that does not count wrongs and is always forgiving. Love counts no wrong. Regardless if someone wronged or hurt you, you have to release the pain, hurt and anger in order to love yourself. Remember in Day Five, we discussed how forgiveness and love are interlinked. Love begins in you for you. The next person cannot do for you what only you can do for yourself. You have to make the decision to heal. Because healing is a process, I encourage you to practice being patient with you. Allow yourself to experience love like you never have before. If you are not sure how to practice what 1st Corinthians 13 is teaching you, ask God to teach you how to love yourself.

Questions:

1. Did you know that loving yourself makes it easier to love others?
2. Do you define love differently after reading 1st Corinthians 13 and its entirety?
3. Write a letter to yourself to express your love for you.

Day Seven

Topic: Love Never Fails

"Let the morning bring me word of your unfailing love, for I have put my trust in you. Show me the way I should go, for you I entrust my life."

Psalm 143:8 NIV

When we come to God, we come to Him because we know He is a God who rewards those who diligently seek Him (Hebrews 11:6). The psalmist was exquisite when he said "Show me the way I should go, for to you I entrust my life." David, the psalmist who wrote the Psalms, was very dependent on God for his daily survival. It was David who wrote, in Psalm 23:1 "the Lord is my shepherd, I shall not want." David's trust in God was so strong that whenever he was to go to war with any tribe or nation, he asked God for direction. He didn't trust in princes…

(Psalm 146:3), but he placed all his trust in God. He rested wholly in God's love for him, in God's eternal salvation. We should do the same.

That is what God wants us to do all the time: Trust in Him because He never fails. Perfect love doesn't promise and fail. The God who gave up His son for our salvation, He will freely give us all things (Romans 8:32). Our trust is not in our abilities to make the right demands, but in His unfailing ability to always provide. God's unfailing love is explicitly mirrored in Christ's death and resurrection. Sometimes we put our hopes in other people while omitting God. We can all take a pattern after David. Because God loves us the most, He will not fail us. I know it seems hard and challenging but getting to know yourself is essential to your survival not only as a Christian but as a woman.

A key to being a woman who loves herself is knowing how to stand firm and confident in God's Word. Romans 3:4 teaches us "...Let God be true, but every man be a liar...". God's word is always true. He never fails! This is our confidence, that God Hears us always (John 11:42), in the same way He heard JESUS when CHRIST was on earth. We are not perturbed by the things around us because we know that God's love Never Fails. 2 Kings

4:26, states, "Run to meet her and ask her, 'Are you all right? Is your husband all right? Is your child alright?'" "Everything is alright," she said. Even when your world is falling apart, you should know, God loves you, you love yourself and all is well. A relationship of love cannot exist without trust.

Questions:

1. Does love begin in you for you? Explain.
2. Why is trust so important to a relationship of love?
3. Do you trust your decision making? If so, is this a sign that you have gotten to know and love yourself?
4. Describe a love in your life that has never failed.
5. Does your confidence in you exemplify your self-love?

Day Eight

Topic: Love Gives Life

"The thief comes only to steal and kill and destroy; I have come that they may have life, and have it abundantly."
John 10:10

Did you know that love is the most powerful force in the world? Love, when given genuinely, infuses us with unknown energy; love gives us life. To grasp the life-giving power of love, let's look at how God, through his only begotten son, Jesus, gave us life. God's love is endless; so enormous that he'd rather his Son die for humanity than humanity perishes. This life-giving power of love is also seen in the lives of mothers with their new-borns.

A mother who just delivered a child can go to any length to see that the baby is well and healthy. New mothers, because of their love, can do anything for their babies. Mothers have natural nurturing instincts for their children, always protecting them from danger. There is a story of a mother who had just recently given birth and was told to me by a friend. This newborn baby girl was just three months old, not old enough to be left alone. But the woman had to quickly pick up some items from the market, so she left her child with the maid in the house.

She was barely ten minutes in the market when she felt something was wrong with the baby. Although she was many miles away from her child, she sensed immediately what was wrong, and quickly called her maid to direct her on what to do. This might sound like a typical maternal instinct story, but it reveals just how much life that love gives us. Perhaps, you have seen a young woman who is newly in love. The glow in her eyes cannot be hidden. Oftentimes, we joke about a new bride looking beautiful, more beautiful than we normally see her. You may wonder, "*Why?*" The reason being is because love brings out the glow in us.

There are scientific explanations on the effect positive emotions have on our psychology. The release of feel-good hormones, the invigorating effect it has on our muscles and all the likes. But most importantly, love energizes with life. When John wrote that God's indwelling spirit gives us life, and gives it to us more abundantly, he was speaking of the spiritual life – the eternal life of God in us. It is most powerful knowing we have the love of God in us.

We have life when we have love! Mothers have strength to fulfil the duties of being a mother when they have love. Wives have peace and joy in being supportive and loving to their husbands because of love. Young women, you have the grace to be gracious and kind because of the love that God has for us and this love also dwells in you. Women are significant in every way. We are special to Christ, and as we are in Christ, we become more powerful because we are then operating in love.

Questions:

1. Regardless if you are single, married, a mother or even a wife with children your daily task should connect you to God's love and plans for your life. How do you see significance in your duties as a woman? Explain.
2. Do you have moments that you feel the love of God dwelling inside of you? If so, explain.
3. What are three goals that you can set to make you more powerful through God's indwelling spirit of love?

Day Nine

Topic: Really; What Does Love Have To Do With It?

"For I am convinced that neither death nor life, neither angels nor demons, neither the present nor the future, nor any powers, neither height nor depth, nor anything else in all creation, will be able to separate us from the love of God that is in Christ Jesus our Lord."

Romans 8:38-39

In Apostle Paul's writing to the church in Rome, he explained to them the unifying power of God in his life. Apostle Paul had gone through a series of trying times, escaping death threats, broken ship at sea and a host of other persecutions. He understood how love can be threatened by hard times and persecutions, but still stand strong irrespective. Many times, in relationships – whether it's romantic or platonic – there will be trying times. There will be days when the emotions will not run as high as we are used to. We will come to points when we will question what we are doing, why we are even in that relationship. But in the end, you may ask yourself, "*What has love got to do with it?*" In response, love has everything to do with it. Yes, everything!

The decision to stay with a person – or even an idea – is birthed from a place of honest love. When these trying times show up, who we are and what we believe in will rear its head (ugly or beautiful). Love has everything to do with it. Love is the life force that helps us stay in a committed marriage even if your spouse is not on their best behavior. Love is what keeps marriages going even when mistakes are made. God's love is the perfect example of what love got to do with it. Before Christ's death, we were sinners, condemned to death. God had no reason to send his Only Begotten son to die for us. But He did. Rom 5:8 teaches us, "While we were yet sinners, Christ died for us." Love has everything to do with what Christ did on the cross for us.

So, you see, love has everything to do with it; from keeping relationships together, to becoming better women daily. We can't go a day as Christians without love. Love is the life we live; it is the life we have been given. We cannot be a Christian without understanding that love has everything to do with our lives and purpose. Any woman who does not understand the power of love, and does not know that love has everything to do with the life we are living will fail at being a Christian and accomplishing what Christ has set out for them to do.

Questions:

1. Do you believe that love can unify a family? Explain why or why not.
2. Have you ever been in love? Was this a relationship ordained by Christ? Explain.
3. List three ways or three roles in which you can use improvement? Explain how love God, you and others will help you to improve.

Day Ten

Topic: Make Love, Not War!

"A time to love, and a time to hate; a time of war, and a time of peace."

Ecclesiastes 3:8 KJV

In today's world, wars exist. At times, we face physical and spiritual wars. We are in times when it feels like everyone is brewing with unseen anger and hatred instead of peace. There are wars, for opposing religion, internal, political; family relationships to list a few. Love can help get us through these difficult times. 1 John 4:16 reads *"And we have known and believed the love God that God has to us. God is love, and he that dwelleth in love dwelleth in God, and God in him."* As a Christian woman, your life should be one of peace and love. Because we dwell in Christ and Christ in God, we have no other life outside the life of love.

Although many wars are going on around you, your home should be your safe place. This is referring to your physical home and your internal spirit. Let's discuss both:

1. Your physical home should be your safe haven. It is the place you find peace and have peace. If you have a husband, decorate your home, cook him warm meals, keep it cleaned and tidy. Place entertainment in the home (television or some sort), and always treat him like a King in the home. Treat your kids as prince and princesses. If you are single, do likewise for you. Make your environment filled with love and peace.

2. Discover your internal peace. You cannot fulfill having a peaceful and loving environment if you are at war with yourself all of the time. **Love you!** Without loving you first as we mentioned in previous days, you will not be able to discover your inner peace. Sister, take time to love yourself, so that you can be good, peaceful and kind to those who are closest to you.

Do your best to never make war with loved ones. Remember, love is not war. The life of God that we've been given means we should always show love, irrespective of the differing opinions we hold. While it may seem difficult to spread love in a world where hate and war is fast becoming the norm, remember that you dwell in God, and because God is love, you radiate love all of the time!

Questions:

1. Showing love is not always easy. Has there been a time recently that you had to pray to show love? If so, explain.
2. Do you see grace in your task of being a woman?
3. What strategy or method do you use to help you connect again to love when you have lost your way? Is it prayer, writing, your children, sports, being social with friends, or something different?

Day Eleven

Topic: I Just Called To Say, "I love you!"

"Others were given in exchange for you. I traded their lives for yours because you are precious to me. You are honored, and I love you."

Isaiah 43:4

In our anchor verse, the Almighty God, expressed His love for the Israelites. He was open about what He felt for them and how He was going to do all He could for them. God was expressive! How often do you tell the people that you love that you love them? Expressing your love should not be so hard, right? But it has become hard being expressive. Some women nowadays see expression as a bad thing, a thing for weak women and people who don't have self-worth. While this is not true, many women tend to hide the best part of themselves and be someone else. Many are afraid of vulnerability or even becoming hurt.

We should have the spirit of freedom, the spirit to be fully and authentically us, and never fear vulnerability. We have the fullness of God to be wholly ourselves. And since our fullness is just like God's, the loving father, let us express our love to the people we love as freely as we want to. Expressing our love does not reduce our self-worth as women. Showing love should not be strenuous and over-thought.

Loving others does not make you weak! Instead, it shows who you are and that you are not shrinking yourself to fit stereotyped societal standards. We have been made for greater! More than what societal defines as woman-ly or feminine. God made us to be the full expression of his person on earth. Therefore, if our God is expressive with his love, which is his nature, why then should you be afraid to be as he is? Call those people that you love, tell them "*I just called to say I love you!*" You are a love being because you are my **Sister In Christ!**

Questions:

1. Have you ever heard the Father say to you, "*I love you?*"
2. When was the last time you thought of a loved one and called them to express that you love them?
3. What would cause you to avoid vulnerability?
4. Have you ever realized that you are truly precious to God?
5. How does knowing that God loves you help you overcome day to day hurdles or troubles?

Day Twelve

Topic: Love Stinks!

"But I say unto you, Love your enemies, bless them that curse you, do good to them that hate you, and pray for them which despitefully use you, and persecute you."
Matthew 5:44 KJV

When we hear about love, especially on social media, we often see a perfect picture of people smiling, laughing, and living their best lives. While social media is an outlet for the picture-perfect definition of love being flawless and filled with happiness, this is not the reality of love. The reality of love is that love is not always about the smiling faces, holding hands, glitz, glamour and perfection as we see on social media. Those are only moments of love. The process of love is filled with challenges and imperfect stories. In fact, it is the many imperfect stories that makes love great.

Because love is something that we work for, it can be appreciated when we finally reach a place in our lives that we can actually love others. Somethings will happen in our lives that will push us so far from love and so close to hate. Sometimes family members and loved ones may walk away. You may have experienced growing up without a mother or father, and have had to struggle in many areas because of the absence of a loved one. If you have been raped or molested, you are or have felt broken. How do you love the one who caused you to feel hate in the first place? This was my initial thought as well. Once I learned what God has asked me to do, I remember hating to have to love beyond reason. I thought to myself, "Love stinks!" Yes, it really does stink because it hurts so bad. The good news is that if and when we get it right, you will then experience freedom like never before.

Sister, let go of the weights that you have been carrying, and release them. The weights of feeling abandoned, forgotten, insecure because life offered you insufficient funds- Let it go! Forget who was not there for you, and remember that Jesus never left you. If you were broken, he was broken with you. If you were hungry, he was hungry with you. And while it hurts so bad that it stinks, if you can let go of whoever wronged you, **LOVE** can heal you. Embrace love not for those who hurt you, but for you! Prepare to live your very best life.

Questions:

1. What is hindrance to your life that prevents you from loving yourself and even others?
2. Have you ever felt hate? What causes hate? What does hate feel like? Does hate create anger or does anger create hate? Explain.
3. Do you believe that God's love for you can heal brokenness, bitterness, hatred and anger?

Day Thirteen

Topic: Live, Laugh & Love

"Whoever pursues righteousness and love finds life, prosperity and honor."

Proverbs 21:21

I have heard people say, "*Life is easy when God is involved!*" I know blank statements such as this make people cringe. People will say things like, "*Life is so hard. Nothing comes easy!*" While there are hard times in life, we cannot and should not dwell on the hardships that we see around us. Our anchor verse says when we pursue righteousness and love, we find life and prosperity and honor. The amplified Bible version makes it even better. "He who earnestly seeks after and craves righteousness, mercy, and loving-kindness will find life in addition to righteousness (uprightness and right standing with God) and Honor.

Philippians 4:8 makes this verse in Proverb more profound as it states, "Whatever is true, whatever is worthy of reverence and is honorable and seemly, whatever is just, whatever is pure, whatever is lovely and gracious, if there is any virtue and excellence, if there is anything worthy of praise, think on and weigh and take account of these things." We are encouraged to always have our minds on pure thoughts, things that edify and make us happy. The Bible is not denying the existence of hard times. The Bible is not teaching us to deny the existence of these tough realities, but to build our faith, so that we only see what God sees; we only say and believe what the word of God says! Are you a woman who hears what God speaks, and as a result, you speak over and into your life? Although troubles are always present, your days should be filled with life, laughter and love.

With God, life is 'sweet' not because there are no challenges, but because we "set our minds and keep them set on what is above (the higher things), not on things on earth (Col3:2 AMP). We see things from Christ's perspective. Living life easy and loving and laughing reflects how we view ourselves in God. It reflects how confident we are on the things God has done and given to us. We are not perturbed by the things happening in the world as these things do not define our reality. Our ultimate reality is defined by who God says we are. Our perfect lives are shaped by what the word of God says. We are the full expression of God's truth.

Are you going through tough times? You will find prosperity and honor because you seek after righteousness. Does life look and feel overwhelming, think of those good and lovely things. Fix your affection on the things above – higher level thinking, beyond what is happening around you. Greater is he that is in you than he that's in the world (1 John 4:4). The Spirit of God in you helps you see life from God's lenses. Seeing life from God's lenses makes life lovelier than what the average person experiences. We have the greater one, the one who makes all things work together for good for them who love God and all are called according to His purpose. Despite what life throws at you, live, laugh and love!

Questions:

1. Have you ever had a moment when life seemed to get the best of you, yet you had to show love and even laughter? Explain how you felt and how you managed to pull yourself together to put the best on the outside.
2. Do you believe that laughter is good for the soul? Why or why not?
3. How often does your family compliment you on your laughter as laughter exemplifies joy?

Day Fourteen

Topic: Love Versus Like

"Love never gives up, never loses faith, is always hopeful, and endures through every circumstance."

1 Corinthians 13:7

The discussion on what separates love from like will forever be an ongoing one. To better understand the difference between *like* and *love*, we need to revisit our definitions of love provided in Day 1 through Day 4. The foundation of every genuine love is inspired by God's love for us and in us. We can't say we love another person when we are still ignorant of what God's love for us is and feels like. We know not to love if we do not know that it is Him who works in us to Will and do His good pleasure.

Here is a list to give us a deeper insight of love:

- Love is sacrificial.
- Love never gives up.
- Love never loses Faith.
- Love is always hopeful.
- Love endures through every circumstance.

The seventh verse of 1 Corinthians exposes us to the characteristics of love. We know what God defines love as and how we have love. But how do we know that what someone – of even us – is showing towards another is love and not just a façade of emotions? The message Bible translation of 1 Corinthians 13:7 strikes a different chord for me. Love "Beareth all things, believeth all things, hopeth all things, endureth all things." What I love the most about this scripture is that love endures. As women, society has conditioned us (forgive me for using the word "conditioned") to always pay back. Seek revenge or even feel validated in wronging someone who has wronged us. We have been taught that when people hurt us, no matter how long ago it was, we must get revenge. Always remember, love and forgiveness are intertwined.

We know that we love someone or that someone loves us when they continuously believe in our goodness despite our many shortcomings. When they/we don't give up on people, it shows that we love them. Love is often the connection that we feel to those who are closest to us.

While love is a strong connotation for family, friends or even people whom we have connected with in life, like is different. The connotation of liking a person or thing implies that we do not have a connection to know them or to know that thing well. In the sense of a person, we like them when we are initially getting to know them. This like or feeling of caring may eventually become love. However, if we *get to know* them and we become no longer interested in them because of their ways or behaviors, we may no longer like them. Liking something or even a person is common, sometimes mutual and not as emotional as love.

There will be people who you will never meet, but may always like! You may like the way they sing, preach, play sports, cook, talk, teach, etc. It is possible to like things without being attached to the thing to the extent of love. As women, we are very connected to our mothers, fathers, and children. Our emotions are normally wrapped up and tied up in them, and this is normal. It is normal to love hard! It is normal to protect, love and pray for the child we birthed. We should never feel guilty for such. While we are doing what is normal, let us reach beyond and do what is hard; love people who we would normally despise enough to like them.

Questions:

1. Do you find yourself at times not liking a person? Oops, it happens. Even as Christian Women, we have those moments.
2. What do you do to protect those whom you love? Do you cover them in prayer? Do you work hard to provide for them?
3. List three things or people you like.
4. List three things or people you love.

Day Fifteen

Topic: Love To Hate

"If a man say, I love God, and hateth his brother, he is a liar: for he that loveth not his brother whom he hath seen, how can he love God whom he hath not seen?"

1 John 4:20 KJV

There is a saying, *"There is a thin line between love and hate."* This saying is rather true because while God commanded us to love, our feelings can alter if we are hurt, broken or if something or someone we love has been destroyed. Remember, we discussed that human love is conditional. Depending on the reason or cause, human love may change! While emotions can change, love should never become hate! The Gospel of John teaches us that we cannot claim to love God, and not love people around us. It is impossible for us to say, *"I love you Lord,"* but hate the person next to you. How possible is it that we love an unseen God – a God we know only by faith, but fail to love the people we see, feel and touch? If we truly love God, we must monitor our feelings towards people on earth to make sure that we do not hate our brothers and sisters. Teach yourself to overlook the wrong that people may do, and to operate in love.

"*God is a good God,*" is a saying that we say all of the time. But is he good enough for you to change the way that you not only view, but also love people? For example, you may recall the story of Zacchaeus. Because of Zacchaeus' social reputation as a tax collector, he was in a disadvantaged position, and was hated by many people. Zacchaeus worked for the government and was always knocking on doors to collect taxes. When Jesus saw him, Jesus did not allow Zacchaeus' social reputation to deny access to His (Jesus) love. Jesus could have walked past him, and reminded him of how much of a social failure he was. Jesus could have told Zacchaeus that he (Zacchaeus) was not fit to be seen with a righteous person like Jesus; however, Jesus did none of that. Jesus showed Zacchaeus love and compassion.

Did you know that Jesus is a loving father although many times, we do not deserve His love? The love Jesus has for us is a gift, and none of us could ever earn His gift of love.

Questions:

1. Have you ever experienced a situation where you felt hate being transformed to love? If so, explain.
2. Have you ever experienced a time when the love you felt for someone was being transformed into hate? If so, explain how you overcame these bad feelings.
3. How do you see the Grace of God exemplified in your life as he is your loving father?

Day Sixteen

Topic: Lovely Day

"This is the day the Lord has made. We will rejoice and be glad in it."

Psalms 118:24 NLT

Each day with Christ should be A Lovely Day. Every day is a new opportunity to be grateful to God! Each day is a new opportunity to express the endless love God has given us; the eternal life he gave us in His Son. When we wake each morning, irrespective of how bad or challenging the previous day was, we should rejoice and declare that this day is blessed. There is a familiar hymn by Joseph Scriven states, *"What a friend we have in Jesus, all our sins and griefs to bear! What a privilege to carry everything to God in prayer! Oh, what peace we often forfeit!*

Oh, what needless pain we bear all because we do not carry everything to God in prayer!" Jesus is a constant friend! We create Lovely Days for ourselves when we can take all of our burdens and concerns to the Lord in prayer.

In the Bible, we see how well David spoke over his life throughout the Book of Psalms. Speaking forth those things that are not as though they were is how we shape our day. Our words become our actions, so words determine if you are setting out to have A Lovely Day. Declare that blessings are falling unto you in pleasant places. Declare that your life is a manifestation of God's life. We will experience A Lovely Day when we speak it into existence. Each day is the Lord's, so we rejoice and are glad in it. Rejoice! We rejoice for each day that God has brought because each new day is a miracle. A fresh chance to experience the fullness of God's endless love for us. God has not only numbered your days, but also, he has desired for you to have the best of days. Rejoice!

Questions:

1. God promises us lovely days. Do you see God's promises being fulfilled in your day to day life?
2. Do you find peace in knowing that you can take all of your troubles to Jesus Christ in prayer?
3. How does having a friend in Jesus create lovelier days for you? Explain.

Day Seventeen

Topic: Love On Top

"Who shall separate us from the love of Christ? Shall trouble or hardship or persecution or famine or nakedness or danger or sword?"
Romans 8:35 NIV

Have you ever wondered about your relationship with Christ? Did it seem that in an ever-moving society and world, you were somehow forgotten? While it may seem hard to believe, Jesus places loving you on the top of his list. There is no doubt that Jesus always places Love On Top. Romans 8:35 teaches us that we can never be separated from the Love of God by anything happening around us. We are forever joined to God's love by His spirit. Christ's love for us is never getting separated by anything in this world! He loves us regardless of what happens. We are always loved by Jesus Christ.

This chapter is a letter that was addressed to the Romans church to assure them of their position in CHRIST. There was an assurance in this letter from Paul to the church in Rome. Paul made them understand that their position as God's beloved was not under threat. Their stand as God's elect was not subject to their actions. It is good to know that we cannot gain and lose our relationship with Jesus. It is always ours! Paul makes it explicitly clear that there was no way God would leave them stranded, all by themselves. He was their ever-present help in time of need. He is God who gave His son freely, so He is able to Give us ALL OTHER THINGS FREELY!

Christ is risen from the grave to give us life and life eternal. It is also important to note Paul's use of language in the 34th verse of Romans 8. He said, *"He died, or rather, he was raised from the dead."* It is Christ's resurrection that seals his Love for us. If Christ had died and did not resurrect, nothing would have changed about us and our nature. It is his resurrection that sealed the deal. It is his resurrection that assures us that nothing can separate us from the Love of Christ.

You might be going through very hard times, slipping and falling. Even in trying times, Jesus Christ loves you and if you seek him, you will experience him placing your Love On Top! Nothing has the power to bring a wedge between you and Christ's love for you.

Questions:

1. Did you know that we are known by God, and loved by him despite what happens?
2. Do we get to pick and choose who and how we love?
3. Do you know that no one is able to drive a wedge between you and Christ's love for you?

Day Eighteen

Topic: Love Heals

"And over all these virtues put on love, which binds them all together in perfect unity."
Colossians 3:14 NIV

Life has a way of causing us to feel broken. Even as believers who are strong and bold in our faith, there comes a time when our walk with God may seem tainted because of the troubles that have broken our spirit. One of the biggest blessings of us being able to experience God's love is how his love heals us. Colossians 3:14 love binds them all in Unity. The word of God is so refreshing in knowing that despite what we have gone through, God's love binds all things together in perfect unity.

To cross reference, this scripture crosses references with Romans 8:28, because it again teaches us that no matter what our obstacles are, good will come from the circumstance.

I encourage you to always be in a position where you can heal. Let go of all past situations! If you find it hard to let go, or even grow to a place of healing, pray and ask the Father to deliver you. While deliverance may not come instantly, and it may take some time, love will heal you. Interestingly, God can allow other people to love you as well and you experience healing through their love for you. Allow yourself to be loved, and Love yourself! You deserve love! You deserve true love! We are healed from all our emotional and psychological pains and scars through love. Love from God, love from others and even the love that we give ourselves will help us to feel good about our lives.

Love is a gift that keeps on giving. Whenever you experience love, it becomes even easier to share that love with others. Being loved teaches us how to love. While someone may have loved you through your pain and helped you to heal, you will do the same for the next person if you pass that same type of genuine love along.

Questions:

1. Have you ever experienced a painful life changing event? If so, how do you recall this circumstance making you feel?
2. What is your most memorable moment of someone loving you through your pain? This someone maybe a family member, church member, friend, spouse, or significant other?
3. How does patience reflect true love?

Day Nineteen

Topic: Beloved

"Whoever does not love does not know God, because God is love."

1 John 4:8 NIV

Throughout this book, **Twenty One Days To Loving Me**, we have learned that God is the standard for love. If you have ever questioned, *"What is love?"* **Twenty One Days To Loving Me** has answered that question. We are made to love because love brings God Glory. When God created us, he gave us his breath. His breath is His essence, His fullness. But after Adam's fall, we became devoid of God's fullness. Christ died to restore us back to God, to be like God. We are like God because we have all that He has. So, if God is love, it means our actions and behaviours should exemplify love. Most of all, love should be in our hearts.

The first point of being a loving person is to know who you are. To know who you are means that you can love other people freely. You are a human being, and you are subject to making mistakes. Despite the mistakes that you make, you are still Christ's beloved. While doing good is great, knowing who you are and that you are always loved by God is more important. God's love and being his **beloved** teaches us who we are. If we do not know we are, we will do the right thing (attempt to love) but with a wrong mindset (want something in return) which makes us give up when the people we are loving do not reciprocate the love.

Beloved, love is not always easy, and is required of us even if it is not given back in return. In Matthew 5:46A, Jesus asks a question, "If you love those who love you, what reward will you get?" Beloved, Jesus wants us to give love when it is reciprocated and when it is not. Remember if you are not walking in love, you are not walking in God's precepts.

Questions:

1. Explain the importance in experiencing God's love for you, and knowing who you are?
2. How does the Holy Spirit reveal God's plan for your life? Is this evidence of God's love for you?
3. What is the most important detail that you have learned so far in **Twenty-One Days To Loving Me** about love?

Day Twenty

Topic: An Overflow Of Love

"Because of the Lord's great love we are not consumed, for his compassions never fail. They are new every morning; great is your faithfulness."

Lamentations 3:22-23 NIV

As you reflect on your journey in **Twenty One Days To Loving Me,** you have encountered powerful tools and tips that will allow the manifestation of God's love in your life. Have you ever heard the saying, "God's love is so wide that you cannot go around, so deep you can't go under and so tall you can't go over?" This saying is true. Jeremiah, the weeping prophet speaks through Lamentations. Judah's judgment drove Jeremiah to consider the grace, mercy, and compassion of God. Despite Judah's judgment, Jeremiah was relentless about the mercies of God. He saw that the monotheistic God loved Judah greatly, and because of his love for Judah they were not consumed.

We too have made many mistakes and done sinful things. However, each morning that we awake, we experience a newness of God's love and mercies towards us. The Lord is faithful in loving us. The purpose of this book is to help you realize how much God loves you, and for you to love him too. As we have previously discussed, love begins with God. Once we love God, he teaches us how to love ourselves, spouses, family, friends and all other people. Love is the key! I encourage you to dwell in a secret place, a place of love. Experience an overflow of love.

As women, we are often naturally caregivers. We are born to give and show love to others. I challenge you to allow an **Overflow Of Love** to flow in you and through you. Love relentlessly, and love others despite their failures and shortcomings. I challenge you to see the good in people even when they do wrong. Keep on loving despite the reasons not to. By loving God and others, you will experience freedom and peace in your heart.

While some people may only do enough, the blessing is in the overflow. There is a blessing in the overflow!

Questions:

1. Explain how love can make you feel free spiritually?
2. How can we experience an **Overflow Of Love**? Can we be so rich in love that we give some of it away, but still have an abundance?
3. Do you believe that an **Overflow Of Love** begins with you understanding how much Jesus loves you? Refer to John 3:16-17, and explain.

Day Twenty-One

Topic: Loving Me Better

"Love the Lord your God with all your heart and with all your soul and with all your mind and with all your strength.' The second is this: 'Love your neighbor as yourself.' There is no commandment greater than these."

Mark 12:30-31 NIV

All of the devotionals in **Twenty One Days To Loving Me** have been essential to teaching you how to love you better! Guess what? If you do not love yourself, no one else may love you. Charity begins at home which means you have to start with God and you! As women, it is vital for us to **LOVE OURSELVES**. Because God works in us to will and do of His Good pleasure, we are meant to Love ourselves. We can become so rich of the love that God has given us that we can richly dispense that love to other people. I have a question for you, "What will people remember about you?" I hope that people will always connect the thought of you to the feelings of love.

You are beautiful! Know who God has made them to be, and radiate that love as freely. You are created for excellence. Love the woman that you are. Love your height, weight, skin color, curves, shape, eyes, nose, etc. Love you some you! Love you to wholeness! Love you to wellness! Did you love yourself and take moments to admire the wonderful attributes that you have to make a statement of gratitude to your creator; these behaviors show God how grateful you are.

In conclusion, thank you for taking this journey with us! I know that you are now prepared to love relentlessly. I know that you will accomplish great things in your family, work career, and in whatever path that you decide to take in life because you will be a beacon of God's light showing his love so freely. As we conclude, I want you to pray this prayer with me:

Prayer To Love

"For the times I aimed and missed,
For the words I said in amiss,
Or even for the moments when I was selfish
And those who mean so much to me,
I failed to cherish.
Father, please forgive me.

Help me on the journey
To see love as my identity.
As in you, there is light
And your light brightens my life.
In moments when I am unsure,
Help me to remember that love is the cure.

Father, love is often the answer.
Help me to be better.
When I do not understand
Because I am human and just a woman,
Teach me your heart
That I may love others without a second thought."

www.ingramcontent.com/pod-product-compliance
Lightning Source LLC
Chambersburg PA
CBHW070106100426
42743CB00012B/2655